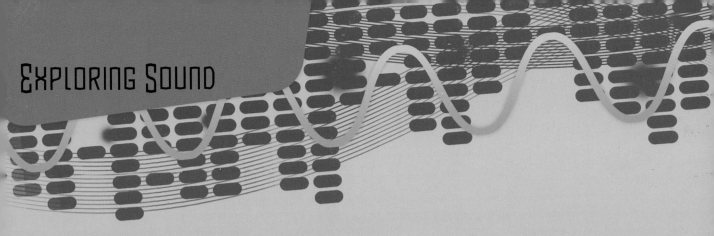

Exploring Sound

Turn It Up! Turn It Down!

Volume

Louise and Richard
Spilsbury

Raintree is an imprint of Capstone Global Library Limited, a company incorporated in England and Wales having its registered office at 7 Pilgrim Street, London, EC4V 6LB – Registered company number: 6695582

www.raintreepublishers.co.uk

myorders@raintreepublishers.co.uk

Text © Capstone Global Library Limited 2014

First published in hardback in 2014

Paperback edition first published in 2015

The moral rights of the proprietor have been asserted.

Edited by Adam Miller, Sian Smith, and Penny West
Designed by Cynthia Akiyoshi
Original illustrations © Capstone Global Library Ltd 2013
Illustrated by HL Studios
Picture research by Elizabeth Alexander
Originated by Capstone Global Library Ltd
Production by Victoria Fitzgerald
Printed and bound in China by Leo Paper Products Ltd

ISBN 978 1 406 27449 3 (hardback)
17 16 15 14 13
10 9 8 7 6 5 4 3 2 1

ISBN 978 1 406 27454 7 (paperback)
18 17 16 15 14
10 9 8 7 6 5 4 3 2 1

Spilsbury, Louise and Richard
Turn It Up! Turn It Down!: Volume (Exploring Sound)
A full catalogue record for this book is available from the British Library.

Acknowledgements
We would like to thank the following for permission to reproduce photographs:
Alamy pp. 5 (© Tim Gainey), 14 (© Blue Jean Images), 23 (© david tipling), 28 (© Joel Douillet); Capstone Publishers (© Karon Dubke) pp. 8, 9, 9, 13, 13, 16, 17, 17, 20, 20, 21, 26, 27, 27; Corbis p. 6 (© Ocean); Getty Images p. 15 (Richard Heathcote); Shutterstock pp. 4 (© Ivica Drusany), 11 (© Maridav), 19 (© Aleksey Stemmer); SuperStock pp. 10 (Chris Cheadle/All Canada Photos), 18 (Hemis.fr), 22 (Juniors), 24 (View Pictures Ltd), 25 (Marka); Design features: Shutterstock © Vass Zoltan, © agsandrew, © Dennis Tokarzewski, © Mikhail Bakunovich, © ALMAGAMI, © DVARG, © luckypic.

Cover photograph reproduced with permission of Getty Images (Bob Ingelhart/E+).

We would like to thank Ann Fullick for her invaluable help in the preparation of this book.

Every effort has been made to contact copyright holders of material reproduced in this book. Any omissions will be rectified in subsequent printings if notice is given to the publishers.

Disclaimer
All the Internet addresses (URLs) given in this book were valid at the time of going to press. However, due to the dynamic nature of the Internet, some addresses may have changed, or sites may have changed or ceased to exist since publication. While the author and publishers regret any inconvenience this may cause readers, no responsibility for any such changes can be accepted by either the author or the publishers.

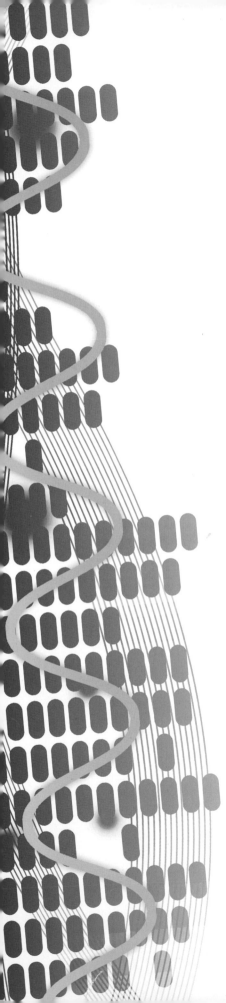

Contents

Some words are shown in **bold**, like this. You can find out what they mean by looking in the glossary.

What is volume?

Has anyone ever asked you to turn down the **volume** on a TV or a music player? Volume describes the amount of sound something makes. Some sounds are quiet or soft – for example, the sound of leaves rustling in the wind. Some sounds are loud, such as the sound of a train pulling into a station or someone drilling in the street. Can you think of some other quiet and loud sounds?

When fireworks explode in the sky, they can make very loud bangs and whistling sounds!

The volume of a sound is important. Loud noises get our attention quickly, so people often use them to warn us of danger. That is why a fire alarm is loud. We speak in loud and soft voices to help us say different things. When we talk loudly, it might mean something is urgent or we are angry. When we whisper, it might mean we have a secret to tell!

Loudest and quietest

One of the loudest sounds we hear is the sound of a plane taking off. One of the quietest is the sound of our own breathing when we are in bed at night.

We whisper quietly so only one person can hear us.

Loud or quiet?

All sounds happen when something **vibrates**. When something vibrates, it moves forwards and backwards very quickly, like a guitar string when you pluck it. When something vibrates, it makes the air around it vibrate, too. These air **vibrations** make parts inside our ears vibrate so we can hear the sounds.

Things that vibrate more make more noise. When we hit a drum gently, it only vibrates a little, so makes a quiet sound. We hit it hard to make bigger vibrations that make louder sounds.

When we hit cymbals hard, they vibrate a lot and make loud sounds!

Sound vibrations travel in patterns that we call **sound waves**. They move up and down like the wave people often do around sports stadiums! These waves are invisible but we can show them as wiggly lines that look like ocean waves.

Firework bangs

When a firework explodes in the air, very hot **gases** push out in all directions. They push so hard they cause big sound waves that make a very loud bang!

These are pictures of sound waves. When something makes big vibrations, it makes loud sounds. When something makes small vibrations, it makes quiet sounds.

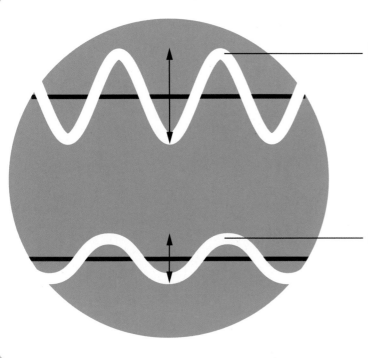

big vibrations = loud sounds

small vibrations = quiet sounds

Activity: Seeing sound waves

Aim different **sound waves** at a target to see what happens.

What to do

1 Stand your tube on the stiff paper. Draw a circle that is wider than the end of the tube. Cut out the circle. Then cut out a circle of the same size from the plastic bag.

What you need
- Plastic bag
- Stiff paper
- Cardboard tube
- Strip of paper 20 centimetres (8 inches) long and 1 centimetre (⅓ inch) wide
- Pencil
- Scissors
- Elastic band
- Sticky tape

2 Make a small hole in the middle of the stiff paper circle with the tip of the pencil. Tape this circle to one end of the tube.

3 Wrap the plastic bag circle over the other end of the tube. Hold it in place with the elastic band to make a drum.

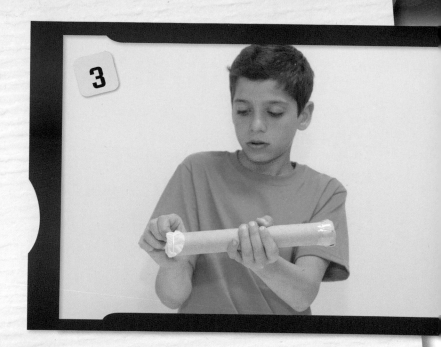

4 Fold the strip of paper in half and tape one end of it to a table. The other end should stick up in the air making an L shape.

5 Hold the tube so the end with the hole is pointing at the top of the paper strip. Tap the drum end of the tube. Then tap it harder. What do you notice?

What happens?

When you tap the drum end of the tube to make a louder sound, you should see the paper move forwards and backwards in a bigger wave.

Getting quieter

Why do sounds get quieter? It's all about **energy**. We use energy to make sounds because energy makes things work and happen. We use more energy to hit a drum hard and make a loud noise. The **sound waves** created have more energy too. This means they can travel further. That is why you can hear loud sounds from far away. Whispers and other quiet sounds do not have as much energy. You have to be closer to hear them.

As things get further away, the sounds they make get quieter.

All sounds get quieter and quieter and then stop. That is because sound energy is wasted as it moves. When a sound wave **vibrates**, it pushes the air in front of it. Then this air pushes the air in front of it. A little bit of sound energy is wasted with each push. The **vibrations** get smaller and the sound gets quieter until the sound stops.

Sound waves get smaller and quieter as the energy is wasted.

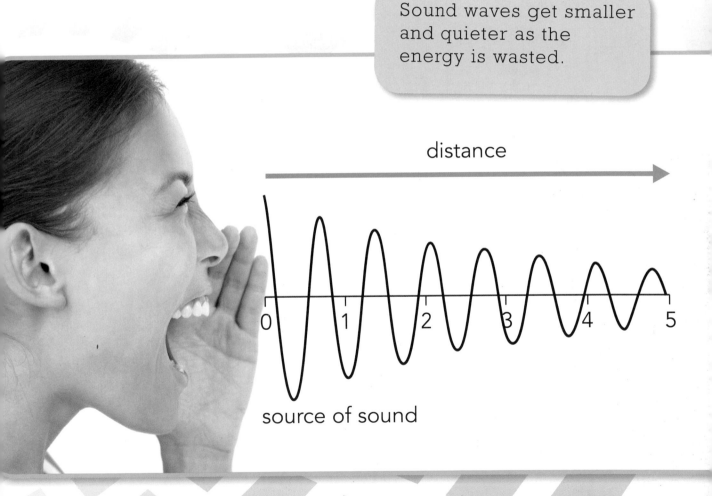

distance

source of sound

Activity: Listen up

Test how sounds lose **energy** and get quieter over distance.

What you need

- One friend
- Tape measure
- Chalk
- Pencil
- Paper
- Ruler
- Set of keys

What to do

1 Mark a starting point on a playground with chalk. Use the tape measure to measure out distances of 5, 10, 15, 20, and 25 metres (or 15, 30, 45, 60, and 75 feet) from your starting point. (You can go further if you like.) Mark the distances with chalk.

2 Draw a table with columns for each of the distances you have marked. Write your name and your friend's name in separate rows below.

	5 metres	10 metres	15 metres	20 metres	25 metres
Name:	could hear the sound very well				
Name:					

3 Stand at the starting point with the set of keys. Ask your friend to stand at the first distance and listen, while you drop the keys on the ground. Ask them to mark on the paper how well they can hear the sound. For example, they could write "could not hear the sound", "could hear the sound quite well", or "could hear the sound very well".

4 Tell your friend to move to the next distance and repeat step 3, until your friend has filled in the space for every distance.

5 Ask your friend to be the key dropper so you can take a turn listening too.

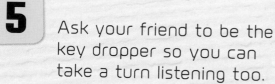

What happens?

When you look at the completed chart, you should see that the dropping keys sound becomes quieter as you and your friend move further away from each other.

Making sounds louder

There are times when we need to make sounds louder so people can hear them from further away. For example, when you see a friend across a crowded street and you want to get their attention. The problem is that when we speak or shout, the **sound waves** that come out of our mouth spread out in all directions.

Why do you think we cup our hands around our mouth to call to someone a long way away?

This trainer uses a megaphone so the rowers can hear him.

SUE   KCS 0

When we make a cone or funnel shape with our hands, we trap the sound waves. This stops them spreading out in all directions. It also helps to squash the sound waves together. This makes them louder and makes them travel further in one direction.

Megaphone masks

A **megaphone** is a funnel-shaped device that makes sounds louder. Around 2,500 years ago, actors in ancient Greek plays wore masks with mouths shaped like megaphones. This helped to make the actors' voices carry further.

Activity: Make a megaphone

Make your own **megaphone** and test how it works.

What you need
- Large sheet of thick paper or thin card
- Large circular plate or bowl
- Pencil
- Scissors
- Sticky tape

What to do

1 Lay the card on a flat surface and tape down the corners. Put the plate or bowl on top of the paper and draw around it with the pencil.

2 Cut out the circle using the scissors. Fold the circle in half and cut along this line.

3 Roll one of the half circles along the straight side until you get a cone shape. Stick the two sides of the cone together with tape.

4 Cut off the narrow tip of the cone to make a mouth hole.

3

5

5 Call to a friend from a distance with and then without the megaphone. Swap places so you can be the listener too.

What happens?

The megaphone helps make the sound louder and sends it in one direction. This is like the way you can twist the nozzle on a hose to make it shoot water out strongly in one direction.

Making music

All musical instruments have parts that **vibrate** to make sound. On a guitar, the strings vibrate and on a drum, the skin vibrates. Instruments also have a part that makes the sounds louder so people can hear them. Trumpets have a cone shape at the end. This makes the air **vibrations** inside the trumpet sound louder when they come out.

Mountain horns

In the past, the alphorn was played by people of the Alps in Switzerland to call each other across the mountains. Alphorns are still played today at festivals. They are usually carved out of wood and some are 4 metres (13 feet) long!

On its own, a vibrating string only makes a quiet sound. Most string instruments have a **solid** surface and a **hollow** space below the strings to make the sound louder. A guitar has a hollow wooden body called a **soundbox**. When the strings vibrate, they make the body vibrate too. When the body vibrates, the air inside it vibrates. This makes stronger **sound waves** that are louder when they come out of the sound hole on the front of the guitar.

The strings on a guitar are attached to a part called a **bridge**. This passes vibrations from the strings onto the body of the guitar.

sound hole

bridge

soundbox

Activity: Make a guitar

Find out how a guitar **soundbox** works.

What you need

- Eight long elastic bands
- Empty cereal box
- Flat piece of card (same size as the cereal box)
- Scissors
- Pencil
- Sticky tape
- Jar

What to do

1 Use tape to seal the open end of the empty box.

2 Lie the box on its back and put the jar in the middle. Draw around the jar. Ask an adult to help you to cut out this circle.

3 Put four elastic bands around the length of the box. Make sure they cover the hole.

4 Put a pencil under the elastic bands near the bottom of the box. This is your **bridge**.

5 Put four elastic bands around the length of the flat piece of cardboard.

6 Strum or pluck the two guitars in the same way. What do you notice about the sounds they make?

What happens?

You should notice that the guitar with the soundbox, sound hole, and bridge makes a louder sound than the flat guitar. The **vibrating** strings on their own make a quiet sound. The **hollow** body of the cereal box helps make those sounds louder.

Animal sounds

Many animals use **hollow** spaces to make sounds louder too. Elephants are the biggest land animals and they make very loud sounds. They are very strong and push lots of air through their long, hollow trunk to make a sound like a trumpet.

Woodpeckers make sounds to call other woodpeckers by tapping on wood with their beaks. They knock on dry, hollow trees or branches because these make the sounds louder. Sometimes woodpeckers knock on the drainpipes of people's homes too!

The trumpeting sounds from an elephant's trunk can be heard by other elephants 4 kilometres (2.5 miles) away.

Noisy monkey!

The howler monkey is the loudest land animal in the world! It blows up its throat pouches and makes a sound that can be heard up to 5 kilometres (3 miles) away.

Kakapo birds are giant parrots that cannot fly. They usually live alone. When male kakapos want to attract a female, they need to make a noise loud enough for the female to hear from far away. They puff up their chests to make a big hollow space filled with air. This helps the kakapo make a booming sound that travels as far as 0.8 kilometers (0.5 miles). Females walk to find the male, following the booming!

Bullfrogs have a special part in their mouths that blows up like a balloon. This works like a **soundbox** to make their croaking sounds very loud.

Reflecting and absorbing

The **volume** of a sound also depends on the things around it. When **sound waves** spread out, they often bump into other things along the way. If they hit a hard, **solid**, and flat surface, such as a wall, they bounce off it. They **reflect** sound waves and this makes the sounds louder. That is why noises sound so loud in a big, empty hall.

The hard, solid panels in this concert hall help to reflect sound waves towards the audience. This helps make the music louder.

Some surfaces **absorb** sound waves. They soak sound waves up like a sponge soaks up water. Soft, bumpy **materials**, such as fabric and rubber, absorb sound waves. That is why a room with carpets, soft seats, and curtains sounds different to an empty room with a wooden floor.

Soundproof rooms

Most bands record music in **soundproof** rooms. These rooms have walls and floors covered with special materials that stop sound escaping. They also stop other sounds getting in. That way, only the sounds of the band get recorded.

Activity: Test sound absorbers

Test some **materials** to see which ones **absorb** the most sound.

What you need
- Radio (with numbers on the volume control knob or button)
- Some different materials such as cardboard, a padded envelope, cotton wool, and old tights or socks
- Plastic freezer bags that you can seal
- Cushion or pillow

What to do

1 Fill each plastic bag with a different material. You will have to cut some to fit, such as the padded envelope and cardboard. The bags should all be filled with roughly the same amount of material. That will make it a fair test. Which material do you think will absorb sound best?

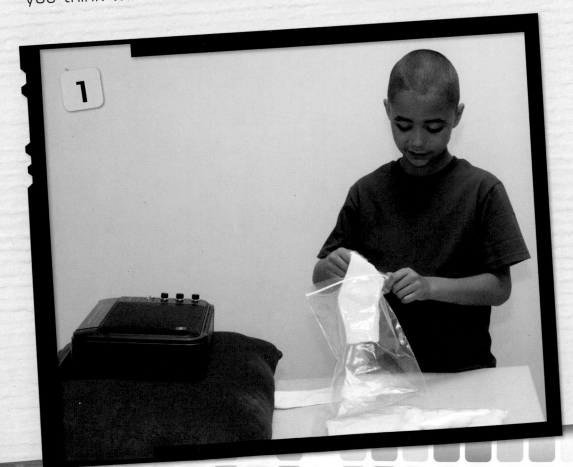

2 Rest the radio on the cushion. Then rest one of the bags of material over the radio speaker (where the sound comes out). Turn the radio down until you cannot hear it anymore. Write down the number **volume** it is set on. If you cannot hear the radio when the volume is high, that material is very good at absorbing sound.

3 Repeat this test with all of the other bags of materials. Which materials block sound well and which do not?

What happens?

The cushion absorbs sound coming from the back of the radio so you only hear sound coming out of the front speaker. It can be tricky to hear the differences, but you should find that some materials absorb sound better than others.

Say no to noise!

Lots of people use sound **absorbers** to protect
their ears. Pilots who fly big jet planes wear special
headphones to stop loud sounds getting into their
ears. That is because very loud sounds can damage
ears and stop people hearing well. Listening to
loud music a lot can hurt ears too. So remember to
keep the **volume** down when you listen to music,
especially if you use earphones. Look after your ears
and say no to too much noise!

Road workers who
use noisy machines,
such as drills, wear
ear protection.

We measure the volume of sound in **decibels**. The quietest sound we can hear is 1 decibel. A quiet whisper is about 30 decibels. A plane taking off is 140 decibels if you are standing near by. People who work where sounds are over 85 decibels wear hearing protection.

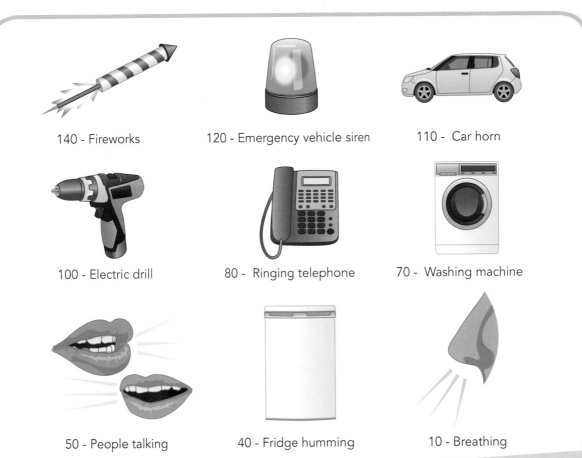

140 - Fireworks

120 - Emergency vehicle siren

110 - Car horn

100 - Electric drill

80 - Ringing telephone

70 - Washing machine

50 - People talking

40 - Fridge humming

10 - Breathing

This picture shows how loud some different sounds are in decibels.

Blast off!

When a space rocket blasts off, it can make a sound that measures 190 decibels. If someone is close by and not wearing hearing protection, this could damage their ears instantly.

Glossary

absorb take something in, for example a sponge absorbs water

bridge small piece of wood on a guitar over which the strings are stretched

decibel unit for measuring how loud a sound is

energy power that makes things work or move

gas thing that has no shape or size of its own. Gases, such as the air in the sky, can spread out in all directions and change their shape to fill any space.

headphones covers over your ears, often used for listening to music. Some help cancel outside noise.

hollow something that has a hole or empty space inside it

material something we use or make other things from, such as wood, rubber, or plastic

megaphone machine that makes someone's voice sound louder

reflect bend or return something, such as sound or light

solid thing that has a definite shape and always takes up the same amount of space. Many solids are hard, such as wood or metal.

sound wave vibration in the air that we hear as sound

soundbox hollow part of a string instrument

soundproof something made so that sounds cannot pass through or into it

vibrate, **vibration** move forwards and backwards or up and down very quickly, again and again

volume loudness of a sound

Find out more

Books

Adventures in Sound (Graphic Science), Emily Sohn (Raintree, 2010)

A Cry in the Dark: Sound and the Science of Survival (Science Adventures), Richard and Louise Spilsbury (Franklin Watts, 2014)

Sound (The Science Detective Investigates), Harriet McGregor (Wayland, 2011)

Sound (Starting Science), Sally Hewitt (Franklin Watts, 2009)

Websites

www.bbc.co.uk/learningzone/clips/vibrations-amplitude-and-sound/7.html
Watch this clip to see how the bigger the vibration, the louder the sound.

www.dangerousdecibels.org/virtualexhibit/2howdowehear.html
You can find out about loud sounds and how they hurt ears on this website.

www.fi.edu/fellows/fellow2/apr99/soundindex.html
You can click on lots of options to find out more about sound and hearing on this website.

www.sciencekids.co.nz/sound.html
There are facts, quizzes, and experiments about making sound on this website.

Index